Wet Wet Wet

PICTURED

Wet Wet Wet

PICTURED

PHOTOGRAPHY BY SIMON FOWLER
TEXT BY MAL PEACHEY
DESIGN BY IDEAS

Virgin

THE BAND

Graeme Clark	Bass
Tommy Cunningham	Drums
Neil Mitchell	Keyboards
Marti Pellow	Vocals
Graeme Duffin	Guitars
Paul Spong	Trumpet
Neil Sidwell	Trombone
Jamie Talbot	Saxophone

Management:
Elliot Davis for The Precious Organisation

First published in 1995
by Virgin Books
an imprint of Virgin Publishing Limited
332 Ladbroke Grove
London W10 5AH

A catalogue record for this book is available from the British Library

The rights of Mal Peachey to be identified as Author of this work have been asserted by him in accordance with the Copyright, Designs and Patents Act 1988

ISBN 1 85227 533 2

Printed and bound by Butler & Tanner Ltd, Frome, Somerset

Designed by IDEAS, Redding, near sunny Falkirk
Photography by Simon Fowler
Simon Fowler would like to thank 'Elliot for putting me forward for the job, Dougie for teaching us about timekeeping, Simon (Scooby) for being my shadow and handing the film to me when I most needed it. Eat To The Beat for feeding Scooby. Brendon and Davey for being there. Liz for taking my photo for the all access pass. Big thanks to the boys for making it an absolute pleasure.'

For Virgin Publishing:
Philip Dodd   Publisher
Carolyn Price   Editor

GRAEME CLARK
PUNKED IN, SOULED OUT

TOMMY CUNNINGHAM
WITH A LITTLE HELP FROM MY FRIENDS

NEIL MITCHELL
SWEET LITTLE MYSTERY

MARTI PELLOW
I CAN GIVE YOU EVERYTHING

ON THE ROAD
SOMEWHERE SOMEHOW

BACKSTAGE
IT'S NOW OR NEVER

LOVE IS
ALL AROUND AND IN THE CROWD

THE WRITING GAME
LIP SERVICE

"The first gig I ever saw was the Ramones and Revillos at the Glasgow Apollo in 1977, on the Rocket To Russia Tour." In the beginning, Wet Wet Wet were a post-punk, industrial rock experience. Graeme Clark, the affable bass player who drives the music-making of the Wets, explains

GRAEME CLARK
PUNKED IN, SOULED OUT

how his love affair with rock was nurtured by his family. "I was 13 years old and had just discovered the Clash, introduced by my older brother who was a guitar player, with a great record collection. I started going through his records, listening to loads of things, picking out what I liked.

"I was a massive Clash fan, and wanted to be Paul Simenon. So I picked up a bass from a second-hand shop for £10. It had three strings on it, was terrible, but almost looked the part because it was a Fender Jazz copy. I learned to play and then, although I felt punk had changed my life, and was the greatest thing to happen to me, in the 80s it just fizzled out."

Unlike Graeme's enthusiam for music, however. As he recalls, "It was always my intention to play music, so I joined loads of bands. The last one was with Neil's cousin Craig Ferguson, who was the drummer. It was a totally pretentious affair, all the lyrics were about Nietzsche and Kierkegaard and that bollocks. The only reason I joined them (their name was Anna Hausen), was because they had a record contract with Human Records, a small independent. They had two singles to record, but this guy who brought me in had actually sacked the original members after the first single. Needless to say, that didn't go anywhere."

Although Graeme had taken a huge step in joining Anna Hausen when, he says, "I left school at 15½ to join the band, convinced that exams weren't going to do me any good at all", he had nothing else to go to. As he saw it, "There was huge unemployment on Clydebank at the time and I just wanted to be a musician. This was my first big chance."

Little did he know then how right that would be. By the time the singer had left, he explains, "Tommy and Neil joined the band." Which signalled a change in musical direction that was as dramatic as the results it brought. "Around the time we were big on ABC because they'd just released Lexicon Of Love and we all loved it. So we thought, forget doing these Magazine covers and pretentious crap, let's write songs with smooth chord changes instead of contrived ones."

So they did, and liked the sound of what they were doing. All they needed was a singer. Which is where a young, apparently shy Mark MacLachlan came in. "One night Neil and I decided that Mark, who we'd gone to school with, could sing, so I called him up and in the understatement of a lifetime he said, 'I don't think I'm up to it'. I said 'Just come up and give it a go'."

Which he did, surprising himself, if not his former schoolpals who knew he could do it. Of course the name had to go, so he became Marti Pellow. Graeme felt settled with the line-up, and so they began rehearsing in earnest. "After that we practised a lot, and did a few covers including Frank and Nancy Sinatra's Something Stupid - we were way ahead of the times, too hip for our own good, really. We decided to spend two years writing, rehearsing, getting ready while other bands we knew were playing the circuit earning money doing Jam songs. Tam was doing some of that, earning a few quid, but the rest of us didn't want to. The aim was always to get a record deal."

Which the determined bass player set out to do in time-honoured fashion. Like so many keen young hopefuls before him, Graeme travelled to the nation's capital to see the record companies.

"I went down to London with a demo tape which we paid £60 to record," he recalls. "I took it to Phonogram and a guy from A&R department said, 'Nah, it's crap. Look lads, if you're going to record a demo, use a good studio.' We were on the dole, we couldn't afford it! I tell you though, it was brilliant going back to this guy after Phonogram had signed us and saying, 'Well, you could have had us for pennies.'" He laughs quietly, then muses, "I don't know where he is now."

"Anyway, on the last day of my trip to London, Geoff Travis at Rough Trade saw the potential. He was setting up a new label, Blanco Y Negro, which he wanted us to record for. But he suggested we use Ranking Roger and Dave Wakeling as producers. I wanted to use Elvis Costello, who'd produced the Bluebells early on, and thought at least he must have some affinity with Glaswegians. But Geoff said he'd book us two days in a studio in Birmingham with Ranking Roger and Dave." At this point, any normal, struggling young band with stardust in their eyes would have jumped on the first available rusting Transit to Brum. But not the Wets. Demonstrating a single-mindedness which would eventually steer them to fame and fortune, Graeme remembers, "When I told the rest of the guys they said, 'It's not exactly awe-inspiring, is it?'"

So they didn't go. But they used the fact that an esteemed record biz mogul had shown interest in them to get gigs, and a manager.

"Geoff came to Glasgow six months later, after we'd met Elliot Davis," Graeme recalls. "At that time Elliot was managing Sunset Gun and running a club on Wednesday nights where bands could just turn up and play, using Sunset's equipment. We took our guitars and drumsticks along and played at the club. Elliot called me a couple of nights later and told me about the management company he wanted to start, asking if he could manage us." The way Graeme remembers it, Elliot was looking to handle bands with as different a sound as possible.

"At the time he was also talking to two other bands. One sounded like Blue Oyster Cult, one sounded like Elvis Costello or the Kinks, and there was us who had a soul kind of thing going. Although to be honest, I never really saw us like that. I never grew up with soul music, I loved the Motown stuff and all that, but I was more into the Clash, Costello and Ramones and rock'n'roll. But Marti's voice had people saying we were a soul band." Which is how a post-punk, industrial rock band named Anna Hausen came to be a multi-million selling soul band named Wet Wet Wet. Or not a soul band exactly!

"Even now I don't think we're just a soul band. I think there's a whole range of stuff in there. There's a bit of country, a bit of bluegrass, a bit of rock'n'roll, a bit of soul, pop. It's all there really."

"We're at that age, right? I've just been out to Toys R Us, to get some toys for the bairns. We had a flight case especially made to put them all in." Drummer Tommy Cunningham is happily married with two kids, a Range Rover and nice home. So how does he manage to keep it

TOMMY CUNNINGHAM
WITH A LITTLE HELP FROM MY FRIENDS

all together while playing in a band who're touring for five months of the year? "It's very hard to have a relationship when you're on the road," Tom begins with some understatement, "so I have a three-week rule where I'm never away from my family for any longer than that.

"If something comes up which means I have to be away too long, I don't do it. Either things get cancelled, or they come to me. I'm determined not to be a casualty of the road.

I don't want to be a fat, 45-year-old baldy with no money, no friends and no family. I want to be 45, fat, bald, wealthy and with all my friends and family around me."

Not that the Cunninghams live out of a tour bus for five months.

"The kids are only on the road with us in Britain", he explains. "In Europe it's too difficult. When we played in Berlin, we had a 12-hour drive overnight to the next venue in Hanover."

So for the rest of the tour it's the Glasgow-family Wets only. Tam, as the others know him, laughs.

"We all know each other very, very well. One look on stage tells us how the other person's feeling. Whether they're overjoyed, pissed off or whatever. We understand each other enough to know when someone needs space. But we all have a wicked sense of humour, too. So although they might need space, we will also pick on them, wind them up, help them out of the mood."

Tommy is a very tactile person, he likes to literally keep in touch with his band mates. He jokes around a lot with them, taking drags from their cigarettes and swigs of their beers. It's all good humoured, even when it's slightly serious, but as he says, these days things are a lot less volatile between them than they used to be.

" As we've grown older we've all become more comfortable with who we are. The roles within the band are much more defined."

As an example, Tommy explains the changes in the way the Wets record.

"In the beginning, at the recording of Wishing I Was Lucky, everyone was in the studio from day one to the very end, so it took five times longer than it should. Now I know when the drums need doing and all the structures are worked out, I can go in and do my job."

Like Marti, Tommy feels the weight of criticism, and explains how he and the rest of the band deal with it.

"I still feel as if it's us against the world. We come together very strongly when people criticise one or all of us. Even though we take ourselves less seriously than we ever did."

For Tommy, the strength of the Wets lies in their unity on and off the road.

"You know," he muses, "I don't think there would be a Wet Wet Wet if one of us left." He recalls how they've all been through the pop star mill, and emerged relatively unscathed.

"When we first began, and we were on TV, it was play acting. The cameras would come on and away we'd go, pretending to be pop stars. But that's not the way to do it, you don't pretend to be who you're not."

Having spent ten years getting used to fame, Tam believes that for him, his life is almost normal. "It's no longer strange to me to know that I can afford a holiday if I want it," he says genuinely. "I don't feel as if I'm being watched all the time wherever I go. Growing up in Glasgow you get the radar early. You know when people are staring at you, wanting to beat you up, or whatever. I used to feel like that all the time I was out when we first started getting successful, but it's disappeared now.

I'm comfortable with what I do. It's my job, I'm in a band, I make music." He shrugs, and wonders at how other bands cope.

"Some bands build themselves personas to hide behind. Wet Wet Wet don't do that. We are the same people you see on TV as you do in the bars and streets of Glasgow or in Safeway. The heaviest weight rests on Marti's shoulders, though. I can go into a bar and three people might say, 'There's that guy who plays in a band', and I can just wave, no-one ever approaches me. But Marti can't go anywhere, not even the toilet, without some guy talking to him.

"A lot of people want to say they gave Marti Pellow a hard time." If Tam's around, however, no-one gets the chance.

"I don't really get recognised that often, Marti gets most of the attention for the obvious reasons. I tend to keep myself to myself." Neil is very much the quiet member of Wet Wet Wet which is just the way he likes it, although he hasn't ever set out to be deliberately enigmatic.

NEIL MITCHELL
SWEET LITTLE MYSTERY

He has a self-effacing sense of humour which can be as dry as the desert. When told that Graeme said of him, "He's as deep as the ocean. I've known him for fifteen years, and he doesn't talk to me much," the keyboard player laughed loudly and replied, "You've got to put that in the book!"

Graeme's remark was made fondly, and Neil understood that. For a band of pop stars, Wet Wet Wet are unlike any other. Their fraternal feeling is genuine and concerned; each member will always look out for the others.

Generally, you expect a 'background' player such as Neil to be jealous of the attention which his very visible, high-profile singer receives. That is certainly not the case with him, or any of the Wets. As Neil explains, "People come up to us and say that our singer is this or that, and we say, 'You don't understand.'

After the shows he stands there with about 40 people surrounding him and there's the three of us surrounded by five, and he has to act the way he does, because he's the centre of attention, all the time. And that's very hard to deal with. I don't know what that's like. We watch him having to deal with it, and we see the state he gets into and that's why we're very protective of him."

Like the rest of the Wets, success has not spoiled Neil Mitchell. He proves, almost against all odds, that it is possible for a pop star to be shy and retiring. He remains at heart the same person he was before fame brought him a higher public profile. Like all of the band, he lives in Glasgow, and says that he doesn't get bothered by people there.

"There's certain places in Glasgow that I wouldn't go to", he explains, "but they're places that you just don't go anyway. I stay in a rather bohemian part of Glasgow where all the students are. They tend to respect you, as do most Glaswegians, and Scottish people in general." The fact that his fellow Glaswegians take most things in their stride seems to Neil to stem from the fact that, "It's to do with the way we're brought up. I think Irish people are similar, as are Scousers, Geordies and so on. We're very down-to-earth, we live in a community and are all friends."

The Wets have now been together for longer than the Beatles managed, and there are no feuds of either a personal or professional nature. There are no teams of lawyers talking to other band members' lawyers about who owns what. As Neil explains, they were friends to begin with, and now, "Wet Wet Wet have been touring together for ten years, and we know each other so well.

After two weeks on the road there really isn't any need to talk at times, you can run out of things to say because it's all been said before. As a band we've actually been together for something like 15 years, since High School. We know each other's good points and bad points and we know how the other guys are gonna feel the next day."

As he sees it, the reason that the Wets have not succumbed to typical pop star failings is to do with, "We have had our rock star moments in the past, but generally we're happy to be doing what we do. It's fairly cliched I know, but we're four lucky guys who've gotten into a good position and we want to ride it out, we don't want to blow it."

So four good friends who have grown up in public stick together, pals for ever. Almost.

"There are times when I could strangle Marti", jokes the piano player, "especially when we're on the round stage performing Goodnight Girl, and Marti comes over to me with the microphone. I get really embarrassed. I really don't want to sing, I hate and detest it. Last night I actually said to him, 'You've got a sick perversion about embarrassing me in front of all these people.' But he still stuck the mike in front of my face. I was mortified. It's not part of the show I greatly enjoy."

Is Neil Mitchell the world's most reluctant pop star?

"I've sat in Memphis Royal studios with Willie Mitchell, man, singing my songs and chatting with him about how things used to be." Graeme Clark is an Elvis Costello fan, Tommy Cunningham likes rock'n'roll, Neil Mitchell is into Burt Bacharach. Want to know where Wet Wet Wet get

MARTI PELLOW
I CAN GIVE YOU EVERYTHING

their soul sound? Listen to Marti Pellow reminisce about recording the band's debut album with legendary soul producer Willie Mitchell, and you get a mental picture of a young Marti wearing white socks and loafers, smiling, grooving in Glasgow clubs to the sound of Al Green in 1978.

"We had Ann Peebles and Carla Thomas cooking for us, joking with us and singing backing vocals. It was a dream come true. Here we were, four 18 year-old Glaswegian lads, never been anywhere, working with Willie Mitchell!"

Marti may have been enamoured by working with Mitchell, but he certainly wasn't in awe. In retrospect, the singer is more amazed by the fact now than he could possibly have been then.

"He turned down Talking Heads and Keith Richards to work with us!" Marti exclaims.

"We were sitting in Glasgow after the record company asked us who we wanted to work with, to produce us, and we said, well, Al Green's producer, let's call him.

In our naïvety we phoned him and he said, 'Sure, send me a tape and I'll see.' He listened to it, called us back and said, 'Let's do it.' He'd listened to Talking Heads and Keef's tapes a few months before ours and said, 'Nah, don't like it.' But he listened to our demo tape and liked what he heard."

The determination to do only what the Wets wanted, which had seen them decline Geoff Travis's offer to record with Ranking Roger and Dave Wakeling when they were unsigned, carried the band to America for the first time. The band's naïvety worked to their advantage, as Marti recalls, "There we were, playing with Willie Mitchell, eating Carla Thomas's stews and going, 'Hey, Willie, how'd you get that guitar sound in 1968?' He'd look at us sideways, squint and say, 'Shit, boy, how old are you anyway?'"

"We weren't actually born then, Willie, but we love that old stuff, make us sound like it." The singer laughs. "So he went into the mixing room at the studio, and tore out loads of digital tape and effects, and stuff from the faders on the desk, threw them all into a big box on the floor, and said, 'Yo Marti, see all that shit? That was gonna distort your voice, now all we got is a bit of reverb and your vocal chords. Ain't that great?'"

Marti throws his arms wide, smiles slightly and continues, "Here we were, working with the man whose big band in 1959 was so hot that Elvis Presley wanted to work with him. Willie's big band was awesome, man. And Elvis used to hang on every word Willie said. Willie told us, 'Elvis used to work in real close to my guitar playing, he'd hang over my shoulder watching my fingers, and then practise exactly what I'd done. He got real good at it.'"

Four teenagers from Clydebank, Glasgow, making music with a legendary figure who taught Elvis to play guitar. Marti is proud of the band's achievements, and a little mystified by critics lack of understanding.

"The music press write about us as if we're this terrible thing, a pop band with no credibility." He pauses. "It used to really wind me up, but these days, I don't care. We sell millions of records, and we really enjoy what we do. Being on stage is what it's all about, watching all those people out there having a good time, singing along and dancing to our songs, that's a great feeling."

As much as he used to protest about the critics' lack of support for the Wets, these days Marti is happy to know that the band give happiness through their music to millions. And as he says, it's great when people simply enjoy what they do.

"When we played the Elvis Tribute Concert in Memphis last year, nobody in the crowd had really heard of us" he says. "Love Is All Around got to Number 41 or something in the American charts, none of our other singles had been hits. And we played after U2, Tony Bennett, Iggy Pop, Kris Kristofferson, loads of great people had done their stuff. It was a real challenge. But they loved us. It was great, the whole crowd were swaying, singing along, gave us a standing ovation. Those people had no preconceived ideas about Wet Wet Wet, they just enjoyed the music we played." The band were so high on the happy side, that after the show they went to see an old friend. "After the gig we went round to Willie's place to say 'Hi', but he wasn't in. What a shame."

He shakes his head and concludes, "Well, maybe I'll never get the credit for being a bloody good singer in a bloody good band but I've worked with some of the best musicians in the world. I work with a great band."

Observant Wets fans will know that, although there

are only four of the band on their album sleeves, there

are always five on stage. That fifth Wet is the quiet,

amiable Graeme Duffin, who is almost disarmingly

ON THE ROAD
SOMEWHERE SOMEHOW

self-effacing, and a constant source of amusement.

A master of accents and funny voices, he can crack the

band up with non-stop monologues between real, and

imagined people, from politicians to other pop stars.

Despite having been with the band since "the fourth gig, before the contract was signed", as he explains, Graeme prefers to be in the background. His performances on stage visibly mark him out as being an extremely important member of the band. This is backed up by the other Wets in private, when any questions about Graeme to them are referred back to him for answer. He's witty, Glaswegian and slightly older than the others.

"Which is why I was not on any of the early single or album covers," he explains, "because the record company wanted to target a teen audience, and I was too old." He laughs, and adds, "I'm not anymore though, am I, Marti?" The singer harrumphs, loudly.

Graeme Clark is a big fan of the guitarist's skills as a musician, as well as his contribution to the band in the studio. "Graeme's great, you don't have to say too much to him about what you want playing, he knows. And he does it, perfectly."

When the band tour, Graeme Duffin is a permanent fixture among them, he travels with the other Wets on their bus, and stays in the same hotel.

The one prime requirement for any hotel the band will stay in is an all-night bar. Since the band usually don't return to their hotel until at least 1 am, there has to be someone around to serve them drinks. One night, desperate for a drink, but faced with a shuttered bar, the band found their way around and behind the grille. A bartender was swiftly found, and he performed his duty with aplomb, despite being under great duress - at one point he had a world-famous pop star poking him in the forehead saying, "I hate spots!"

A piano in the bar is a big plus. One morning at 4 am with the sun coming up, trombone player Neil was tinkling the ivories, making jazzy type sounds, when Marti decided to sit behind him on the piano stool. Marti then plonked away at the upper scale of the keyboard. Neil played Tom Waits' I Beg Your Pardon, Dear in an attempt to get Marti to sing rather than play, but after two verses, Marti once again began tinkling. Until, that is, he fell off the stool. At which point Dave, Marti's personal bodyguard, decided his charge needed to go to bed.

Quiet, Irish and a former hairdresser according to Marti, Dave is a kickboxer who works out each morning regardless of what time he gets to bed the night before. And he only goes to sleep when he knows Marti is tucked up.

Dave's boss, and head of security on the tour, is Brendan, a rock security veteran, who travels everywhere with the band, staying in their hotel, riding on their bus. He's obviously completely at ease with the band, almost one of them. He's also a great joker.

Marti has a necessarily good relationship with both the security men, and the singer likes to take the mickey out of Dave. Marti tells the following story with great relish. "The other day in the gym, Dave's kickboxing, getting his feet way up above my head height, and Brendan's standing there looking unimpressed. When Dave's finished, Brendan says to him, 'Come on then, have a kick at me', so Dave, mucking around, aims a kick above Brendan's head. All of a sudden, Brendan stood on Dave's trailing foot and picked him up, threw him over his shoulder, and started running around the gym. It was so funny."

Besides playing jokes on each other, the main source of on road entertainment comes from the ever-present games console. It's the centre of attention in the dressing room, and the tour bus. The whole band play Tetrus, with varying degrees of success.

"I started playing it first, and then the other lads got into it," explains Tommy, "now we play games against each other. The other night the photographer for this book, Simon Fowler, had a go and wiped us all out! He's now got the highest score so far. He's a demon on it! Came out on a one-night stand and beat us all. We won't be using him again!"

"I can't stand it," claims Graeme. "Neil's pretty good," says Marti. "It drives me mad," the keyboard player confesses.

However, when it comes to more physical games, Neil is a more than willing participant. Especially for the odd game of football.

Most the band are avid Rangers fans. This includes Dougie Souness, the band's formidable Tour Manager, who explains how he got hired: "I used to play drums in a band that rehearsed in a studio next to them, back before they were famous. We supported the same football team."

The band used to play regular, competitive games against the crew. Until, Graeme explains, "The last time we played, Neil's keyboard technician fell on him and nearly broke his nose. Poor Neil's nose just swelled up. One of the papers ran a story saying that Marti did it!"

Although all the band enjoy the game, it's Marti and Graeme who are fanatical Rangers fans. "I was a huge Davie Cooper fan," says Marti, "He was so good. Forget Best or Gazza, Davie could do amazing things with a football. I remember Ally McCoist telling me a story of how in a game for Rangers, Davie beat a couple of defenders and then laid a perfect pass to McCoist's feet who just had to put it in the net, which he did. As he ran up to Davie to be congratulated, Davie said, 'Was the Mitre sign facing up at you when it got to you?' He was so funny."

"The thing about West of Scotland lads is," explains Graeme, "as soon as they can stand they get a football put at their feet and they get the strip and all that. So, of course I love football. When I went to watch Davie Cooper in 1976 at Clydebank that was it, I was as knocked out by it as I was later by music."

There are various footballs to be found kicking around backstage at a Wets gig. But don't try to kick Dougie's. "This is my personal ball, it's my stress-release mechanism," he smiles. "If you come down a corridor and I'm blasting this ball against a wall, don't get involved."

It's little wonder that Dougie sometimes needs stress-release. The All Around And In The Crowd Tour was not only the biggest that the band had undertaken, but it was also technically the most complex. And it was put together by Dougie. He has been tour manager for the Wets for the last eight years, and is the highest authority on the tour, the man that everyone answers to.

One sunny afternoon as the world-famous Wets relaxed on the lawn of an exclusive hotel, nursing hangovers and deciding that they wouldn't soundcheck, Dougie appeared in shorts and vest, mobile phone as ever at his side. "Right", he barked in his powerful Glaswegian brogue, "you'll all be on the bus at 4.30 for soundcheck, right."

And they were.

Being responsible for the smooth running of a multi-million pound enterprise is not easy, but Dougie seems unbothered by the fact that 65 crew and eight musicians depend daily on him.

"Touring is a team game. It's not about individuals, I link band, management, record company, crew and so on. I make sure the sound people are working with the lighting crew, not against them. I have had to let some people go because I didn't think they had the right attitude, and I do have some

strict rules, the main one being no alcohol while working. I have given people red cards for that."

Because there are some 38 tonnes of equipment in the air, safety measures have to be strict. "Oh aye," Dougie confirms, "last February I had to take all my crew on a Health and Safety tour, visiting every venue, where we'd meet with the local police, fire brigade, and venue's technical and security staff. Because this is the largest structure to ever be hung above a rock crowd's head, everything had to be double checked. I had a 50-page health and security document which everyone got, and had to read. I had to think of every risk and how to avoid them." Always a man to give credit where it's due, Dougie singled out the crew members who deserve a special mention:

"Jimmy Innes my production manager, Milan Rackic the stage manager, Jimmy Ebdon the sound engineer and Chris Beale at the sound company, Terry Lee and Geoff Grainger from Light & Sound Design, Phil Broad the head rigger who's responsible for putting all that stuff in the air every night, and Brendan Hyland the security manager."

All Around was truly a team effort.

With the endless round of bland hotel rooms and inter-changeable venues, having some physical semblance of continuity around, something recognisably belonging to the Wets, is extremely

BACKSTAGE
IT'S NOW OR NEVER

important. To avoid the feelings of displacement brought about by constant travelling, there are items which go everywhere with the band, and which help make them feel at home, no matter where they are.

"*Most venues have comfortable furniture backstage these days,*" *says Dougie, adding,* "*but we bring our own TV, video, stereo and games console.*" *For Dougie and the rest of the crew, each venue backstage area has to become their office.*

And so, as he explains, "Because I have to actually work in the venues, I have a travelling office of phones, computers, faxes, printers, all that kind of stuff, which are packed into a couple of flight cases. We use about a dozen small rooms backstage as management offices, production office, crew room, interview room, band dressing room, make-up room, brass dressing room, family room, and so on."

The band's dressing room is the one place in which they will spend most of their time at the venue before and after the gig. Its layout is therefore extremely important. The room is always large, with a sofa, two armchairs, a stereo and video console in a flightcase, a table laden with fruit, sandwiches, fruit juice, coffee and so on. Two ice buckets sit beside it full of soft drinks and Holsten Pils ("They sponsor the bar", explains Graeme).

Beind the door is a clothes rail with several suits hanging neatly in line. Marti's mustard yellow crushed velvet outfit is complemented by a dark blue one of the same cut. He'll change into the blue one after the show. "I get all my suits made by a little old guy in Soho," the singer explains, "he used to make them for the Krays in the 50s. He's great, I must have about 35 of his by now."

The rest of the band are slightly more soberly attired. Something which Graeme Duffin finds a little sad. "I won't stand out like Marti", he half-jokes. Tommy tries to persuade him that his suit is just as smart, and much more refined. Graeme doesn't look convinced. But then, he has his guitars hand-made to order.

On a small table by the suits sit various aftershaves, colognes and hair gels. "Look at that", Marti points to a large bottle of Ralph Lauren's Safari aftershave. "That's Tommy's. Sad, eh? Here's a great aftershave!" He picks up a royal blue, cylindrical box with Trumper written in gold script on it. "Churchill used to have this guy make his aftershave. It's really peppery. I love it."

Off the back of the room are showers and toilets, imperative for the band as they have to clean up after two hours or more on stage, under red hot lights. Once showered and changed, the band will make their way along the corridor after the gig to the ever-present Wet Wet Wet bar.

The pre-gig routine for the Wets differs from day to day, mood to mood, city to city. None of the band have particular routines that they have to follow, and as Tommy says, "Some guys don't want kids around before they go on stage, they like to have silence before going out. Others want music blasting. And I like to go and sit with my family."

Marti, meanwhile, will "Do some voice warming up exercises, take a shower, lounge around."

And Graeme will often "Play some Tetrus maybe, wander around, talking to people."

Neil's different. Try asking him anything pre-gig and you'll probably get, "Can I talk to you later?"

Very often, competition winners in each city are brought backstage to meet the band. All of the Wets make sure they're in the room, smiling, ready to meet them. The band pose for pictures, answer questions, and are nice to their fans, a lot of whom give the band hand-made cards. Marti picked one out. "Hey, spooky", he turns to Neil. "She put a unicorn on it." Marti has a unicorn tattooed on his left shoulder. "It was a drunken dare", he smiles.

For the two hours or so between soundcheck and performance, the band and friends mill in and around their dressing room.

But with half an hour to go before show time, everyone is ushered out by Brendan, and the door is closed. They're not disturbed.

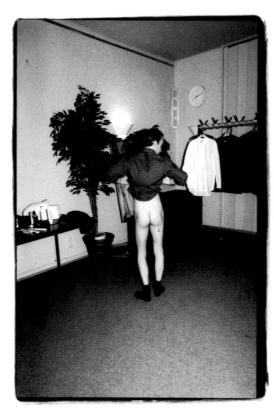

The All Around Tour was the largest that Wet Wet Wet ever undertook. They covered more territories and earned more air miles in eight months than they

LOVE IS
ALL AROUND AND
IN THE CROWD

had for years. The reasons why they put themselves through such a gruelling schedule are many. But for each of the band there is one universal reason: they love it!

As Tommy sees it, "For me, playing live is where I get to express myself, and every three minute song is a chance to play differently. It's spontaneous, and happens in an instant. That's the way it should be."

Graeme exclaims honestly, "I love playing live, it's what it's all about. I love the fact that after a couple of weeks we get so musically tight that we don't need to talk while we're playing, we just feel it. A look between us gets the message across."

Marti might sound cliched when he claims, "It's the greatest feeling," but then he adds, "There might be nights when I feel terrible in the dressing room, that I really don't want to go on. But there's no way you can say to 12,000 people, 'Look, I don't feel too much like singing, so could you come back tomorrow?' So I go out to do the show. And every time I immediately feel great, like I'm on top of the world."

Despite playing so many gigs on one tour, the band are disciplined about what they play. Boredom is not an issue it seems, as Tommy explains, "The crowd keep things spontaneous, keep us on our toes. We should change the set around maybe, and sometimes we'll throw something in, but usually we kept to the set list." Neil adds, "To begin with on the tour, especially in Europe, when we were playing a lot of slow numbers people were having difficulty with it. But we're kind of stubborn and didn't change the set to put in some faster numbers. Either they'd take it or leave it."

Of course people took it, and loved it, too. Or mostly, as Neil explains. "Actually, in Europe a few reviewers slagged us off for the bit in the show when Marti gets all of us to sing, saying it was a bit like Karaoke, which I thought was pretty spot-on." But then, he would say that, wouldn't he?

Tommy has no such quibbles about the tour, he's unequivocally enthusiastic.

"That was a fabulous tour," he states plainly. "We played bigger arenas, to larger audiences, and a different audience too. Early on in the tour, in Germany I think it was, for the first time I heard the audience singing along with Goodnight Girl, sounding like a Welsh male voice choir instead of the usual girly one."

Tommy has perhaps the best take on the whole show. Summing it up for the Wets, he says, "The watchword for me is entertainment. It's not how cool you can be, or how big your car is. It's 10,000 people coming to see you play, and hopefully after two hours going away saying, 'Wow, that was amazing'. Let them escape for a while, don't remind them how horrible the world is, or how different you are, how much money you earn. I don't think we do that, I think we say, 'Hi, how you doing? Let's have a party'."

A major part of any arena tour, where it can be difficult to create an atmosphere, is the set design. Given that most of the venues are vast, aircraft-hangar buildings with the ambience of a big shed, the focal point of the stage is extra important. For the All Around set, Tommy hoped to create a semblance of "a TV set we did in Europe. I thought it looked great and wanted to do something like it." So the stage was draped with white curtains, each separate level was marked by bare lightbulbs, each instrument had its own space on differing levels. "We worked on it over a couple of months, putting in not just walkways but drum stands and so on," explains the drummer. "When you think about it, there's only so many places that you can put drums, keyboards, horns etc., but we tried to do as much as we could within the normal boundaries. What we didn't want was for it to look square, we wanted it to look lopsided."

The highlight of the All Around And In The Crowd set, of course, was the catwalk, which would be dropped into place and raised again at strategic moments.

"The catwalk is a stunning idea, and although we're not unique in having two sets and a way to get the band from one stage to another, I don't think anyone before has used a floating catwalk like this", enthuses Tommy, with good reason. "For 15 years of drumming I've been the guy at the back, and playing in the round everyone's on the same level. I love it."

All of the Wets share Tommy's enthusiasm for the In The Round stage. The original idea came from tour manager Dougie Souness, who explains, "Since 1988 we've played arenas, but last year the boys told me they wanted to do something different. Initially I wanted them to play in the round, but the band weren't totally keen on that idea, although they liked it. So I came up with the idea of a second stage and catwalk." Not in itself a unique idea, as Dougie confirms, however, "What's unique about this set-up is how the band get from stage one to two. I was aware that other bands, such as Bon Jovi for instance, had done something similar, but their catwalk was fixed. Take That, Simply Red and Peter Gabriel all used something similar. But in comparison to all the other catwalks, this is very different and much bigger. The catwalk itself weighs nine tonnes and is lowered and raised by something like 72 pulleys. We've had to increase the crew a bit, from the usual 40-45, to 60-65, and it takes 10 trucks to move the whole show."

The band obviously enjoy the chance to run along the catwalk, playing to separate, usually distant parts of the crowd. "I love getting to the people in the seats at the side of the arena," confirms Graeme. "It feels as if they're close enough to touch."

Once on stage two however, when the catwalk has ascended to its station in the rafters, and the trio of Marti, Graeme and Graeme Duffin take equal centre-stage, everything changes.

Somehow the vast shed of a venue feels as if it's transformed to a small, intimate club. As Graeme Clark strums the opening chords of Little Feat's Roll Um Easy on his acoustic guitar, Graeme Duffin prepares the bottle-neck for his electric acoustic.

Up to this point in the show, Graeme's contribution has been vast. He sings backing vocals, dances around with his guitar played expertly and cleanly. Now, however, he comes to the fore. The song is a quiet ballad, heavily dependent on the colour which the slide guitar provides as it mirrors the melody.

Graeme claims that he 'wings' it, kind of plays it from memory, in which case he has a perfect recall. It's almost note-for-note, the same as the original (to be found on Little Feat's Dixie Chicken album).

The Wets have always performed a lot of other people's songs both live and in the studio. For this tour they ended the shows with The Beatles' All You Need Is Love.

The vast range of musical influences at work in Wet Wet Wet, are given full rein In The Round, not only in the cover songs they perform, but in the 'Karaoke' bit as Neil calls it. "I usually sing Al Green's Let's Stay Together, Tommy sings Every Breath You Take, Graeme will change what he sings fairly often. But then, Graeme's into Little Feat, I like Frank Sinatra, Marti likes Al Green and Tommy's a rock'n'roll guy.

There's all those ingredients and from that we'll pick out the songs we do. We'll all play each other stuff and try to get them to like it. Sometimes it works, of course, sometimes it doesn't." Marti will also reveal that his earliest memory of music is being four years old, at his grandmother's house where, "On a Sunday she'd start her old Radiogram up, and play Dean Martin's That's Amore on 78 rpm, some Nat King Cole, all that stuff. Dino was so cool."

Watching Marti on the Round stage, images of Elvis's comeback special TV show from 1968 are evoked, especially the segment with The King, Scotty, Charlie and DJ sitting opposite each other, as Marti straddles his chair, stands with one leg on it, leans his head back and almost croons.

By the time Tommy and Neil are lifted from beneath onto the stage, fans standing around the edges of the round stage are in ecstasy, and as the Wets tear into With A Little Help From My Friends, every mouth in the building is shaping the words.

"It's only a shame that we couldn't have the Round stage on every gig," laments Graeme, "but it was just too big for some of the European venues, so only the British crowds got it. But we loved doing it."

As each of the band are constantly stating, they have been together for almost 15 years, and they are obviously good friends. There was a time when they would fight each other in order to settle disputes. But that time is past, according to the band's manager Elliot Davis. "I was renowned for being the most

THE WRITING GAME
L I P S E R V I C E

verbally aggressive in the early days. But over the years I've deferred to others in the band. Now we have other ways of venting our anger and settling our grievances. Still sometimes, however, people make the wrong decisions and have to be told that they have."

One subject on which all of the Wets agree is that of the critics. Marti might be blasé about the reviews and features which get written about the band in public, but in private it still hurts. As Neil admits, "Criticism does upset you, but we're a bit long in the tooth now, and we've had criticism for a long while. Some of it's right and a lot of it's well off the mark, but that's their job: to criticise. And I don't think people are going to remember their reviews, I think they'll remember our shows and our songs. Having said that, the reviews of Picture This and the gigs have been pretty good."

Elliot Davis agrees that the critics seem to be warming to his band, but, he says, "I think the critics' problem with the Wets is that in the beginning they slagged the band off so badly and now that they are starting to see how good the band actually is, it sticks in their throat," he says simply. "They can't bring themselves to admit that they are on the record as hating the Wets but now think they're quite good. The journalists are not for turning! But they're beginning to revise their initial impressions and to rewrite history. Marti might say he doesn't care but he does. We've all become very thick skinned over this, as you have too, but it still hurts."

Graeme shrugs his shoulders, and states simply that, "Commercial success and critical acclaim are almost incompatible in this country."

Tommy feels that, "We think we're a credible band, the press think we're not. Personally it used to wind me up something rotten that we were always criticised and no matter what we did, or do, we're not given the credit we deserve. Now, I think the band as a whole have reached the point where we think, 'So what? Get on with it.' It really hurt that after our first album, Popped In, Souled Out, we were slagged off as just another pop band. We shouldn't still be around, should we? Yet here we are after 15 years together and eight years of success."

Like everything the band do, writing songs is a joint effort. However, according to their manager, one member takes more responsibility for creating new material than the others.

"Graeme starts the process, ends it and is there throughout," says Elliot. "The others come in and do their bit and add their ideas."

Graeme offers the explanation that, "From the beginning we always wanted to write songs which would lend themselves to having strings on them. Our strong point is melody. We get the chord structure down first and then bang our heads against the wall trying to get a melody. Somebody will come up with a riff, or sometimes a whole song, but the music usually comes first and then Marti will start making noises to the tune, la-la-la, that sort of thing. Sometimes it comes really quickly, and at others it takes ages."

The process for the last album was slightly different, however. As the bassist explains:

"For Picture This we wrote songs in our usual way, the tune kind of forms itself among us, the words are shaped around the tune. We asked Elvis Costello if he wanted to work with us, but he was too busy so he put us onto Chris Difford from Squeeze. He said he'd like to, so he came up to Glasgow, and he had this lap-top computer full of 300 songs or so. He said, 'Here's a list of the titles, take a look and choose one, then I'll call up the words for you.' It was great working with him, and it was a different way of working for us."

Wet Wet Wet

7 great reasons to GET WET

POPPED IN SOULED OUT
Released 28th April 1987
Highest chart position 1

THE MEMPHIS SESSIONS
Released 7th November 1988
Highest chart position 3

HOLDING BACK THE RIVER
Released 30th October 1989
Highest chart position 2

HIGH ON THE HAPPY SIDE
Released 27th January 1992
Highest chart position 1

LIVE AT ROYAL ALBERT HA
Released 17th May 1993
Highest chart position 10

PICTURE THIS
Released 17th April 1995
Highest chart position 1
Featuring the smash hit
singles:
Love Is All Around
Julia Says
Don't Want To Forgive You Now
Somewhere Somehow

END OF PART ONE -
THEIR GREATEST HI
Released 8th November 19
Highest chart position 1